Whispers of her Soul

Grace Luman

Presentation by *BookLeaf Publishing*

Web: www.bookleafpub.com

E-mail: info@bookleafpub.com

ISBN: 9789357214278

First edition 2023

Back From

Ebb and flow
Push and shove
Light and shade
Camouflage veil

Endless spectrum
A spec in time
Bound by infinity
Death by forgotten light

Soul starvation
Body overload
Filled to the brim
Destructive overflow

Endless cycle
Invisible chains
Fear ripe for the picking
Shallow gains

Rise and fall
Stumble and crawl
Through the trenches we go
Dignity left at the door

Keep it going
Mend the mask
Dust it off
Punishment harsh

Emotional assassination
The final blow
Crack, smash, shatter
Dinner and a show

Pivot, spin, turn
Confusion rife
Gentle caress
Ego takes the knife

Clock ticks down
The final push
Push comes to shove
Never enough

Bullets fire
Arrows rain
Wrap me up
In your blanket of shame

Spiral and flail
Crash and burn
Fuel on the fire
Futile yearn

Infinite protrusion
Push and twist
Mute volition
Silent wish

Rise from the ashes
Release the spurs
Light up the shadows
Bone below fur

Down rabbit down
Lion above
Underestimation
You only think you have

No turning back
Nowhere to hide
Nothing to lose
Leap and rise

Rise you shall
Like an Angel of light
Skylit radiation
Flightless flight

Internal knowing
Intuition rising up
Flow within me now
Wrap me up

Final glance
Into the shadowland
Can't see you now
Far below you stand

No Sir, Not I
For I am soaring high
Watch me glow
Reverie of perfect light

Dance and shine
Crown fastened tight
Free Floating
Illumination bright

Turn up the volume
Fireworks a-flight
Admire from a distance
Untouchable delight

Cosmic karma
Authentic life
Sweet relief
Butterfly's flight

Yellow brick road
Golden fleece
Peace in time
Breath release

Undone

Impalpable truths sear amidst depths of Souls
alight
Let the incomprehensible words billow and fall
Expelled from the raw, fleshy wounds
As they form these melodies on white washed
stains

Only after you have submerged into the darkest
depths
Bounded and restrained, thrashing and gaping
Only once you have waded and dredged, and
clawed, and suffocated
Drowned, and revived, and floundered, and
crawled

Only after you emerge through
All dripping and broken
Only then, my scraped and bleeding heart
Will you truly know the reasons

Let me purge this sweet release
Fill me up, all my cracks and creases
Overflow the hollows of my core
With the essence of your untouchable frequency

Flood my vessels and veins
With your infinite expanse
To the beat of your heart
My body aches to dance

Allow me to keep these jagged
Edges, and scar tissue reminders
And know they do not deter
But rather do serve

As fuel to perpetuate
Illuminate the reminder
Of true self form
New ways to be kinder

For I have come undone
And accepted all layers
A deluge of your Divinity
Every shade, in all the colours

Weeping Love and dripping Hearts

Something broke, I cry
In the night I look for you
Are gone. Release me

Sleepwalking

The light I see in you
Is the light I feel in me

The light I feel in all
Reverberates right through me

Everything connected
But we fail to see

We look with our eyes
And our egos seek

Within, without
External hunger rife

Attached but disconnected
Hunger equals strife

You ask all the right questions
But you never really try

So you stay within the circle lines
And wonder why I cry

Rat race, fast paced
Never slowing down

Distraction, dissatisfaction
It never makes a sound

Brainwash, mind mush
You never stood a chance

Take a peek, look behind
Daggers at a glance

Shackled chains, glass ceilings
Sliced by diamonds, sparkling

White beards, shut it down
Threat alert, too shiny

Push hard, play fast
They always grind it down

Untouchable desires
Sought, but never found

It's the intricate design
It's just what they Intended

Give them a tiny taste
Too blind to be offended

Divide and conquer
The seeds are planted young

The horizon's getting smaller
But you turn around and run

You've missed the point
The ship is sailing

You should be kicking strokes
But you're sinking and flailing

Endless cycle
Merry-go-round

Floating Vertigo
Bubbled up in sound

Fear is your base line
Shame is your name

Perfection your weapon
Ready, aim, blame

Deflect, Sweet distraction
Round and round we go

Slow burn, build up
Pressure cooker, blow

Never want to go
To the depths you need to go

Refusing the reflection
U-Turn at every option

Mesmerise me
Fire burning bright

Camouflage chameleon
Change colour in the light

Thick fog swirling
Blindfolded in the night

If only you'd go through
You'd emerge all draped in Might

But you sit up on your high horse
All armored in your whites

Oblivion shades the shadow
So you'll never see the light

Futile, breathless
Energy critically low

Heart shaped, Soul rape
You leave me all alone

I hear the whispers cry
Their echoes in the wind

I want to run and help
But you cut off both my feet

Getting louder now
Kick her while she's down

Warfare of the mind
Wash, rinse, repeat

Insanity

I feel the pin drop through every sound
A tip so sharp, only my eyes can see as it glitters
in the flames

It's game on now, show your weapon
May these bloodless bullets leave no mark
Silent wounds remain unseen

Death by a thousand paper cuts
Each one a badge of honour
She's the Martyr of the hour
Her sacrifices fall by the wayside

Shine the light through the cracks
Intentions of pure illumination
Irrespective of the why
Futile attempts drain the essence of being

Pin cushion heart bears no blood
Invisible stains cannot be cleansed by these salty
drops
I create my canvas with your poison of choice
A mere vessel

A goat for your offering
Sleeves rolled up
The stalk before the pounce
Eye of the storm

Rock, sway, duck, and roll
Head bowed low
Curtsey and retreat

Defenceless blows
The quiet chaos

The tip of the dagger glistening
I can look beyond to the prequel

Soul space
Floating without an anchor
The rust of the chain was too thick for it to
handle
The frequency too low to bear the weight
Higher it rises, harder it falls

Ignite the ignition
Madness creeps back but it never really left
Subtle undercurrent
One slice too many

No light
No shade
Grey dominates

Inside this suppressed limbo
Release atop the mountain peak

Ever present circles
Spin and scratch
Here and now
But nowhere to be seen
Vigilante senses take the helm

Tear it down and grate it bare
No remains but the flesh of an angel
Wrap me in her weightless wings

I beg

Through

Each time I think I
Might just feel some peace

This feeling creeps back
It won't leave me be

Each time I think I
Can finally glimpse light

This darkness pokes at me
Leering and ready to fight

I try to do the things
I know I need to do

But this push leaves me breathless
A resistance so cruel

I ache, and I cry, and I wish, and I pray
I rest, and I weep, and I try and meditate

And through all it I grow
Just a tiny bit each day

I'll try and keep the monster
From coming out to play

I really want to run
Dance, and have fun

But this ache in my heart
Turns everything to mud

Sometimes it catches me
So hard and so fast

I don't know what hit me
How long is this going to last

It likes to dig in deep
So hard and so tight

I'm so tired from all the weight
Bones aching from this fight

I try to keep my face up
Towards the shining light

Find glimpses of joy
And remember my Might

Trying to heal this body
Heart, mind and soul

I'm reminded to go slow
I've had to learn how to crawl

I've stumbled terribly hard
Along the cobbled way

Had the wind punched out of me
Every fucking day

But I'm moving on through
With as much dignity and grace

I can possibly muster
In this terrifying space

And as I gradually reclaim
My vital energy flow

I'll dance once again
I'll find my glow

And one glorious day
All grateful and smiling

I know I'll look back
All my light shining

Because I will remember
The depths that I went to

To emerge here illuminated
I had to go right through

Lusus Naturae

This stench of uncertainty
Is strangling me
This screaming silence
Is killing me slowly

It invades and consumes
An incessant drumming beat
Permeates and infiltrates
I can't think, eat, or sleep

You want to carve me to shape
But my grain is too thick
Try to smooth my edges out
They're too sharp, much too slick

You desire to mold
My pliable pieces
But I am unyielding
And we are opposing species

You slice my skin
But I don't bleed
Pierce my flesh
These wounds refuse to speak

Your love once inspired the best in me
Now my best looks like a Hyde
So here I am, helpless at your feet

Your voice once lit my insides up
With butterflies it glowed so bright
So here I kneel, broken at your feet

Now that gorgeous sound of mine
It has become my Kryptonite
So down I lay, lifeless at your feet

Inevitably
My organs flood
Eventually
My insides drown

Infinite spiral
Pull me down
There is no light
I cannot be found

The tumultuous waves we sail

An ocean of tears
Each salty drop reminds me
To go with the flow

Presopolis

A truth proclaimed cannot be unknown
Words uttered cannot be unspoken
Choices made cannot be undone
After your action is set into motion

Choose gracefully, My King
Your people are weeping

Expectations weigh heavy, responsibilities
burden
But your army you refuse, drop down the curtain
Respect and honour, sliced thinly down to size
Pride and ego dominate this demise

Choose wisely my King
Your Kingdom is crumbling

In the name of the Crown I give myself to thee
And if I am not worthy, crucify me
Permission granted, willingly
For you I'll sacrifice, every part of me

Choose bravely, My King
Your castle is burning

You can be any King, that you choose to be
But you don't know why you're fighting, you're
too blind to see
All the power you possess, infinitely
That got lost with the demons and raged the seas

Choose Lovingly, My King
Your heart is drowning

Full Swing

Finally, from the depths
I am yellow and rising
Far longer than expected
Grapple releasing
In slow motion
I am unfolding
Transformation's a funny thing
I feel the projections
Watch as the storm clouds
Ascend with Thor's anger
I'll be the one
Releasing bolts of thunder
May the lightning shoot fire
From these droplets of shame
That shatter my insides
And crush all my flame
But the burning amber
Can never distinguish
The embers of soul
This fire is fierce
It'll gleam through till dawn
As tears trickle down
Dusty cheeks
All hopeless and drawn
From it all, will rise

The phoenix from ash
Strong and unstoppable
Ascension in a flash
It's different this time
I feel the shift
Like a trembling Earthquake
It slammed me full hit
I've tried to keep grip
Of my balance and grace
I've stumbled and slipped
And buried my face
But I am here now
Back full swing
Achingly glorious
Are these fragile wings

Violoncel

My beautiful instrument
An extension of all that is me
You allow me to release
All that longs
To no longer remain
So tightly suppressed
So deeply confined
Set free all that is
And all that wants to be
All that is buried
Unheard in the deep
Expressed with the rhythm
Exhale, descend
When no trace of oxygen
Is sought in these lungs
You are my Air
My Beat
And my Love
Vibrations mingle
Energies intertwine
Together we invoke magic
Light up stars till they shine
The creation of sound
The sound of creation
Angel wings enveloped

In blissful free floating
Carried fourth to stir up
Waves of emotions
And feelings forgotten
Long lost in the motions
To muddy your comfort
And serve to remind you
That biding your time
Is no longer an option
Let the notes of this soul
And the voice of this truth
Serve to propel
Carry and move you
For here and now
Is all that we are
Right here
Right now
Is all that we
Have

Mother

Seasons change, come full
Circle of life, infinite
Love, beauty surrounds

Pieces

I feel so betrayed
I feel so broken

You've stripped me bare
You ripped me to pieces

You put me together
Just to do it again

Sew me up
Just to tear me open

You do not get to say
That I did not try

Because trying for all of you
Cost more than my life

Trying to get to you
Trying to bring you to

Trying to find you
Trying to reach you

Trying to pull you free
Trying to keep you with me

Took nearly every last breath
From this Earthly body

I gave you every piece
All my patience and my love

I gave you every ounce
All the light that I possessed

I gave you every shred
Of everything I ever had

You took it all
You bled me clean

You sucked me dry
You drained my life

All my energy
All my grace

You took it all
Didn't look twice

How could you do it?
Leave me broken on the floor ?

How could this love of Angels
Turn to a hell I've not known before

I believed that not one thing
In this world could ever break

All we were, all we had
All our dreams that were ours to make

Now here we are
No more, nothing left

I've had to leave you behind
I can forgive but not forget

I built my whole world around you
Spent half my life next to you

So, at night, my Soul
She visits you

And when the burning sun rises
I cry for you

There's an exhaustion in my bones
That doesn't want to leave

And hands around my throat
That just want to squeeze

This burning in my lungs
Is begging for sweet air

These dark crimson stains
Have left me raw and bare

And so it begins
The long, gruelling process

I'll drag myself up
Slowly regain focus

I'll get up off this floor
Put myself back together

Once more I'll stand tall
Instead of laying here helpless

And the glue that I'll use
To put back the pieces

Will be dripped in gold
Infuse all these creases

Limbo

Eyelids flutter
Heart walls unfurl
Brick by brick
Whispers transpire
Becoming what always was
Come full circle
High frequency decimals
Reach a fever pitch
Unbound me from
Your fearful lack
Directionless delusions
Press the petal on your ego
Forgotten truth
Pure being
Touch long lost
Flutter against screens
Inner scrapings
Act as reminders
Banging shutters
Incessant ramble
Deliberate drowning
Domination of the echos
Fade back to silence
Forgotten but not lost
Ignored but not silent

Struggle recycled
Till the day
Truth transpires

Circle Edges

Why don't you just
Unlock the gate?

You hold the key
Your freedom awaits

But the mangled twists
Of the Crown's thorn thicken

Screaming resistance
Power shrinking

The sparkle of shackles
Like moth to flame

The outer layers shiny
But it always stays the same

Undesirable desires
Temporary high

Destructive arrivals
Circle edges tight

Gold plated mesh
Translucent, opaque

Unaligned intentions
Bear fruit in the dark

Conduction of self
Reconstruction not needed

There aren't any holes
But you never believe it

What you fail to notice
You're too blind to see

You look with your eyes
But your heart cannot breath

What will it take?
Not lost, but not found

It quietly screams
It whispers in shrieks

Listen louder
Listen hard

It's a sound you can hear
Through only your heart

Conversations with God

37

Submerged, inundate
Me, wrap me up. Unfurl me
Within, flow through me

Be

The dying art of doing
Absolutely, sweet nothing
To simply sit with yourself
With your breath, and your being

To feel the flow
Which connects us to all
Each and every living
Creature, great and small

Connection creates
The unspeakable in us
Something no human words
Can ever truly express

It's a feeling, a knowing
A call from within
A whisper a flutter,
Floating on the wind

It can be felt in a hug
So much more than just
Limbs intertwined
A surging of hearts

The rhythm itself
A force of nature
Of life, of love
Of hope and adventure

It is inside the womb
Of every Mother, alike
Who gives her all
To create space for new life

First within herself,
Then Earthbound
She will smile through her tears
And sing through her pain

Because all her exhaustion
Aches and her sorrows
Are nothing compared
To that which glows

Illuminates blindly
Shines so brightly
For something far greater
Than just her alone

A mere spec are we
But there's a force which resides
Within and without
We cannot deny

It flows through everything
Each mountain and leaf
Through every delectable sound
Of Nature's Melodies

A droplet of water
That is the flowing seas
All the lakes and the rivers
The oceans and creeks

A spectacular snowflake
Sparkling crystalline
Trillions an avalanche makes
And forms lands of ice

Each drop, every seed
An imperative role to play
Miraculous by design
A true masterpiece

So slow down, take a breath
Take a moment to be
To feel all you are
All that is, and just be

Scar Tissue Heart

Finally, a moment of respite
The multiverse of raging whispers
Seem to have released their grasp
If only just for a moment

Rising silence as numbness subsides
And although it flattens in an alternate state
Perhaps tomorrow the day will ascend and
exhale
Without the crushing weight

Inside the belly of the familiar darkness
Which tempts to swallow every fibre of being
Glimpses caught of higher light
Skins ache to bathe in your glow

She reminds herself, and she is reminded
Not of what is, but always was
And so begins the gradual reclamation
Each and every bruised and battered shard

Tiny smooth pieces, pointed, and sharp
Eyes closed, irrespective of time and distance
A cracked and broken vase
On display, for those who bear witness

And as she emerges through to the dawn
Squinting at the blazing glare
Soaked and dripping liquid
Her thirst will never be quenched

Because knowledge is ascension
Source, an unstoppable expansion
Creation is infinite
Elevation, a force unpreventable

And the love she possesses,
Internally
Can never be contained
Suppressed, or forced easily

Or bound by the thick
Gravelly walls
Constructed unconsciously
By needles and threads

Woven with sorrow
And moments of joy
They work, tiresomely
To build what she thinks

She must do to please
Her artwork framed
Woven tapestries
Which never can reflect

Truly, really
All this is
And all that is
Yet to exist
And yet to be

Born from the wreckage
Of her stories and scars
Free, but bound always
By her Scar Tissue Heart

Struggles of the Psyche

The sadness that is
The weight that invades
Forces its way in
Uninvited
Unrequited
Armour up
The battle begins
The familiar stench
Of a war zone rife
With dust and smoke
Illusions dominate
Eradication of practices
Will lost to the wild
Retreat into otherworldly
While gravity bears its teeth
Bliss be gone

Wash away my Earthly stains

45

Light rays, bluest hues
Walls of ice melt away. Purge
My oceans. Cleanse me

Whispers of her Soul

Success attached to the physical
Is doomed to fail
Because the petals of happiness
Cannot bloom in the shadow

The seeds of truth
Can never grow
When laid in a bed
From the soil of ego

Because the Ego's sole mission
Is to keep you be
Prevent you from danger
But from a place of full of fear

Because the pain of the world
Cannot touch you there
But, Safe in your box,
Through your walls you can't see

Blocked by your shadows
You've denied your essence
You've Silenced your child
And abandoned her there

Ignorance is bliss
But you know you can hear it
When the moon shines white
There're times you can't refuse it

In the dark of the night
She's begging to be heard
Aching to take flight
How much longer will it take

Before you open your eyes
And face the reflections
Finally take action
And not just bare witness

To the faraway
And forever distant
But infinitely, ever present
Whispers of her soul